What do we think about
Disability?

Jillian Powell

WAYLAND

Titles in the series

What do we think about …

Alcohol   **Disability**

Bullying   **Drugs**

Death   **Family Break-Up**

Find Wayland on the Internet at http://www.wayland.co.uk

All Wayland books encourage children to read and help them improve their literacy.

 The contents page, page numbers, headings and index help locate specific pieces of information.

 The glossary reinforces alphabetic knowledge and extends vocabulary.

 The further information section suggests other books dealing with the same subject.

✓ Find out more about how this book is specifically relevant to the National Literacy Strategy on page 31.

Editors: Carron Brown/ Kim Protheroe
Consultant: John Bennett, a Health Education Coordinator
Cover designer: Jan Sterling
Designer: Jean Wheeler
Photo stylist: Gina Brown
Production controller: Carol Titchener

British Library Cataloguing in Publication Data
Powell, Jillian
What do we think about disability?
1. Handicapped – Juvenile literature.
2. Sociology of disability – Juvenile literature
I. Title II. Disability
305.9'0816

ISBN 0 7502 2209 3

Picture acknowledgements
The publishers gratefully acknowledge the following for allowing their pictures to be reproduced in this book: Martyn F. Chillmaid, *cover, contents page*, 18, 19; Sally and Richard Greenhill 4, 5, 8, 9 (top), 10, 11, 12, 15, 22, 24, 25, 26, 27; A. Blackburn *title page* , 6; C.F.C.L/Image Select 7; Chris Schwarz 9; Impact/Peter Arkell 13 /John Coleman 14, 20 /Simon Shepherd 17, /Dave Young 23; Getty Images'/Jon Riley 16.

First published in 1998 by Wayland Publishers Limited, 61 Western Road, Hove, East Sussex BN3 1JD

© 1998 Wayland Publishers Ltd

Printed and bound by Eurografica in Vincenza, Italy.

Contents

What is disability?

We are all different. We all have different abilities. There are things we can do, and things we can't do.

Disability means not being able to do some things. When someone is disabled, there are some things they cannot do.

Who is disabled?

One in ten people in the world is disabled. Sometimes you can tell that someone is disabled. Other times it is not so clear.

Disabled people are like everyone else.
They have their own ideas and feelings.
They have things they like doing.
But they have special needs.

Why are some people disabled?

Some people are born disabled. Some disabilities can be passed from parents to their children. Other people become disabled because of an illness or accident.

Some people become
disabled when they
get old. Other people
are disabled for a
while because they
have hurt themselves
in an accident.

What does physical disability mean?

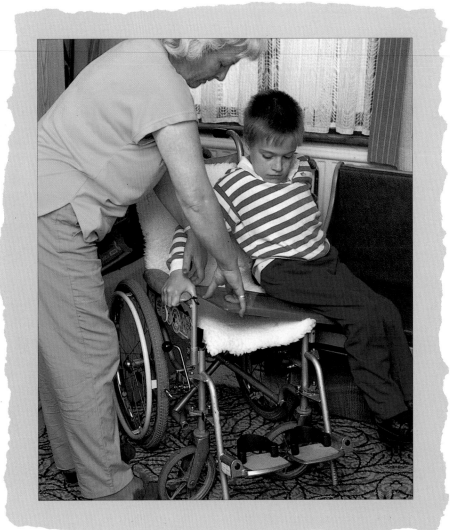

When someone is physically disabled, some parts of their body do not work very well. They may not be able to move parts of their body.

A person who is blind cannot see. A person who is totally deaf cannot hear at all.

Sally can't hear very well. So she needs to wear a hearing aid.

How does it feel to be disabled?

People who are disabled have special needs. They may feel they have to try harder or work harder than others.

They want to try out lots of different things, to find out how many things they are able to do.

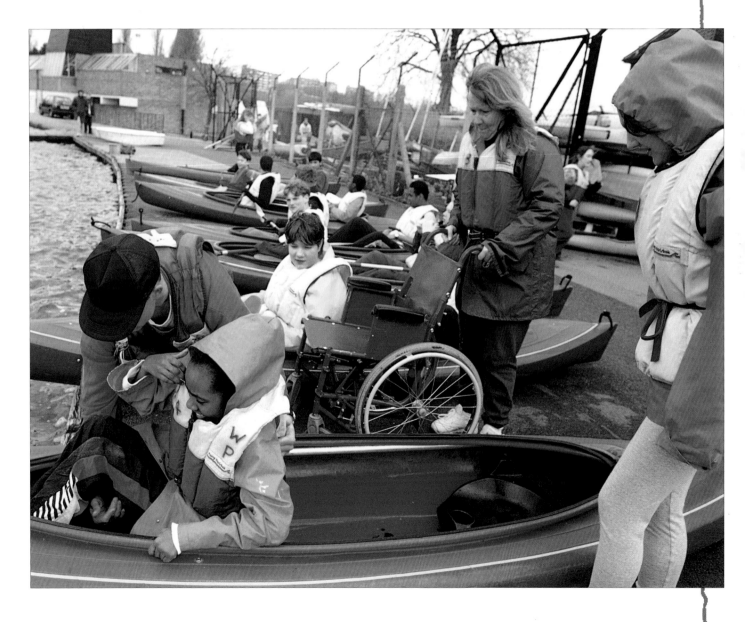

How can things be made easier for disabled people?

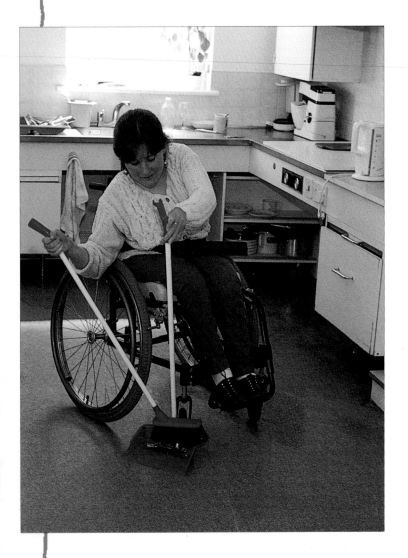

Some disabled people need wheelchairs to get around. They need to be able to move around and reach things easily.

Sometimes, changes need to be made to their homes to make everyday life easier for them.

People in wheelchairs can find it
difficult to move around buildings
that have stairs.

Lifts and ramps can make it easier to
get around. Wide doorways help too.

Can disabled people work?

Many disabled people are able to work. Like everyone, they have different skills and abilities. But because of their special needs, it can sometimes be hard for a person with a disability to find a job.

This blind woman has a guide dog to help her get to and from work. Without her dog she would find it difficult to find a job.

Can we do anything to help people who are disabled?

We should do our best to be friends with one another and help each other. It is wrong to treat disabled people differently from other people. It is also wrong to ignore people who are disabled, or call them names.

By spending time with people who are disabled, we can get to know them properly. We can find out what they think and feel about all sorts of things.

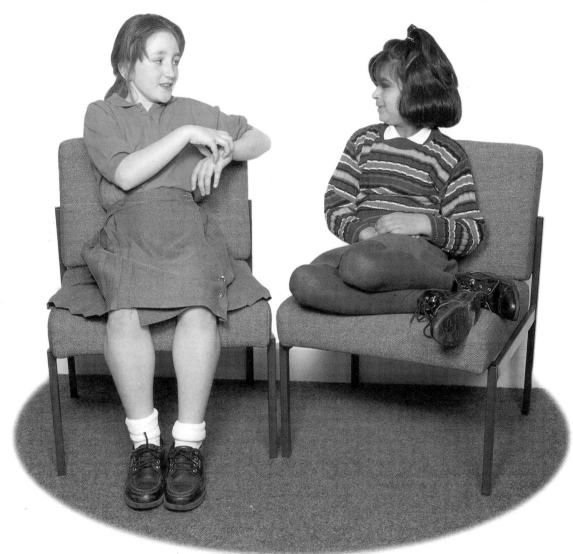

Kirsty learned sign language so that she could talk to her friend Gita, who is deaf.

What other kinds of help are there for disabled people?

Science and technology have both helped to make life easier for everyone. Computers can help some disabled people and explain what they think or how they feel.

Some people who are blind use Braille to read. They learn to know words by touch.

Guide dogs help people who are blind to get around safely.

Joanna's guide dog lets her know when it is safe to cross the road.

Can people who are disabled enjoy sports?

People who are disabled can take part in many kinds of sport. They can enjoy water sports such as swimming and sailing. They can play team games such as wheelchair basketball or rugby.

People who are disabled can take part in
sports competitions and races. Some
sports have been designed especially for
disabled people.

Wheelchair races are very popular.

Where can disabled people meet friends?

Like everyone else, people who are disabled can make friends at school or meet new people by joining clubs and groups.

Joe met a lot of new friends when he joined a youth group. Joe and his friends enjoy the same kind of music. They also like to play table tennis together.

How are disabled people special?

We are all different and we are all special.
We all have different things to give and
to share with each other.

Disabled people have special needs,
but this does not stop them enjoying life.
Like everyone, disabled people enjoy
being themselves.

Notes for parents and teachers

Read this book with children one to one or in groups. Ask them what kinds of disability they have heard about. Do they know anyone who is disabled?

Try awareness exercises such as closing their eyes or covering their ears. Ask them how they feel, and if any of their other senses seem sharper.

Ask the children to think of something they do every day, such as a task or a journey. How easy would it be for someone in a wheelchair? What would need to be changed?

Talk about the way buildings can be changed to make things easier for people with disabilities. Include changes needed at home in rooms such as bathrooms and kitchens. Ask the children to think about any changes they would make at school to make things easier.

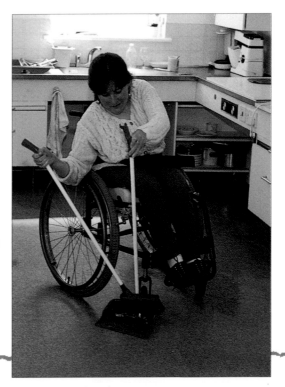

Disability charities or self-help groups may be willing to send someone to talk to the children. A talk on lip-reading and sign language could start a discussion about ways of communicating with each other when we cannot rely on words.

Ask the children what words they associate with someone who is disabled. It is important that they understand that name calling and using words such as 'spastic' as an insult to others are unacceptable.

Talk about the kinds of treatment that some people with disabilities need, for example physiotherapy or kidney dialysis.

Talk about the kinds of disability people can have when they get older. Explain that in old age, some parts of our bodies can begin to wear out. Ask them if they know any old people who are disabled.

Talk about the Paralympic Games and some famous disabled achievers, in sports and other fields, such as, Beethoven, Helen Keller and Christy Brown.

Glossary

Abilities Things people are able to do.

Braille A kind of writing that uses raised dots, so that blind people can read by touching.

Hearing aid Something worn by deaf people to help them hear.

Sign language A way of talking to people by making signs with your hands.

Skills Things people are good at doing.

Special needs Extra help that some people need.

Further information

Books to read

Let's Talk About Disabled People by Pete Sanders (Watts, 1997)
We're Talking About Disability by Jenny Bryan (Wayland, 1996)

Organizations to contact:

RADAR (Royal Association for Disability and Rehabilitation)
Unit 12, City Forum, 250 City Road, London EC1V 8AF
Tel: 0171 250 3222

The Royal National Institute for the Blind
224 Great Portland Street, London W1A 4WW
Tel: 0171 388 1266

The Royal National Institute for Deaf People
19–23 Featherstone Street, London EC1Y 8SL
Tel: 0171 296 8000

Scope (for people with cerebral palsy)
12 Park Crescent, London W1N 4EQ
Tel: 0171 636 5020
Helpline: 0800 626216

Use this book for teaching literacy

This book can help you in the literacy hour in the following ways:

 Children can learn to read non-fiction books and understand that the reader can select according to what information is needed.

 They can use the questions raised in each chapter to gather more information from other sources.

 They can compare this book with fictional stories about disability to show how similar information can be presented in different ways.

 They can try rewriting some of the situations described in the form of a story, letter or news report.

Index